VOGUE ON

RALPH LAUREN

Kathleen Baird-Murray

ABRAMS IMAGE
New York

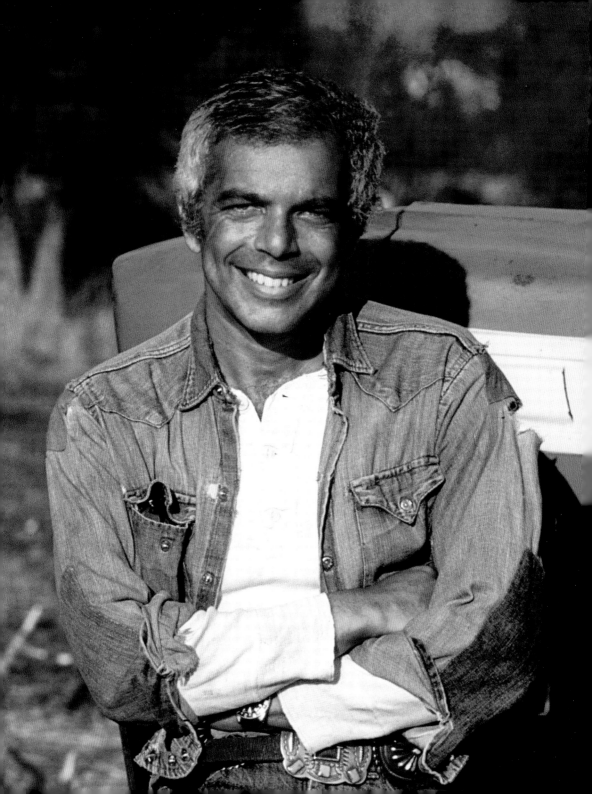

Born in the USA: Ralph Lauren's well-worn denims are trademarks of his unmistakable American ease.

page 1 *A sketch from Lauren's 1978 Western wear collections; relaxed cowboy clothes that feel authentic.*

previous page *Naomi Campbell and Christy Turlington bring a touch of sequinned glamour to a Ralph Lauren classic: the nautical stripe. Photographed by Arthur Elgort for American Vogue, 1992.*

"RALPH HAS CREATED A WORLD
THAT YOU FEEL YOU CAN ENTER
WHEN YOU BUY SOMETHING
BEARING HIS NAME, WHETHER
THAT BE A PAIR OF JEANS,
BLANKET, A COAT OR A PAIR
OF SOCKS."

ALEXANDRA SHULMAN

Born in the USA: Ralph Lauren's well-worn denims are trademarks of his unmistakable American ease.

page 1 *A sketch from Lauren's 1978 Western wear collections; relaxed cowboy clothes that feel authentic.*

previous page *Naomi Campbell and Christy Turlington bring a touch of sequinned glamour to a Ralph Lauren classic: the nautical stripe. Photographed by Arthur Elgort for American Vogue, 1992.*

"RALPH HAS CREATED A WORLD
THAT YOU FEEL YOU CAN ENTER
WHEN YOU BUY SOMETHING
BEARING HIS NAME, WHETHER
THAT BE A PAIR OF JEANS,
BLANKET, A COAT OR A PAIR
OF SOCKS."

ALEXANDRA SHULMAN

EVERYBODY'S
ALL AMERICAN

The year was 2007, the city, Moscow, and a pair of gold scissors sat on a small white box, waiting to cut the blue satin ribbon that stretched across the front of the three-story, 1870s mansion. Television crews, paparazzi, reporters, and guests waited excitedly in Tretyakovsky Passage, trying to steal a peek inside the new 8,000-square-foot (740-square-meter) Ralph Lauren store replete with glittering chandeliers, their largest accessories department, and enough Ralph Lauren memorabilia to satisfy the most zealous of fans. Having flown in with an entourage from New York, the eponymous owner, tanned and silver haired, stood at the entrance with Ricky his wife of (then) 42 years who looked enviably svelte in a gold-embroidered tuxedo. Two of their three children, David and Dylan, accompanied them on either side. The cameras flashed, The gold scissors cut the ribbon, the crowd cheered, and Ralph Lauren Moscow was officially open.

For anyone wondering how this all began, how a tie salesman from the Bronx could end up heading a global corporation netting $7 billion in 2012 alone, the answer was inside the store. Beyond the Ricky handbags, the paint, the perfume, the pillowcases, and the covetable Collection evening gowns, lay a pile of neatly folded soft cotton polo shirts in an array of rainbow colors. On the left breast of each shirt sat an emblem of a man on a horse with a polo mallet raised high in the air. Both endearing and enigmatic, Ralph Lauren's inimitable polo-player logo was internationally almost as well-known as that other symbol of all-America: Coca-Cola. As British *Vogue* wrote in 1999, the logo and the brand it stood for had become "a blueprint for the label-as-global-presence." The opening in Moscow was the sixth flagship store and came 40 years after the inception of the house.

Renowned for its classic aesthetic yet with an unnerving ability to capture the essence of what people want before they even know it, a Ralph Lauren collection has always had a basic premise: "to offer something to wear when life demands clothes that feel good but don't make you look like you're trying too hard." (Joan Juliet Buck, American *Vogue*, 1992). Credited with creating the lifestyle concept, Lauren has never been about fashion for fashion's sake: his are clothes

The dream Lauren lifestyle at the beach: Ralph and Ricky with their sons in 1978, photographed by Les Goldberg.

"THE CLOTHES OF RALPH LAUREN ARE A FORM OF CINEMA, THEY FULFILL THE PRIVATE FUNCTION KNOWN IN MOVIES AS THE BACK STORY."

JOAN JULIET BUCK

Tailored suiting with feminine appeal. Lauren introduced the concept of sportswear with a small "s," as seen in this photograph by Mike Reinhardt for American Vogue, 1974.

overleaf Hurrah for the Hussar! A velvet jacket and velvet stretch leggings reference Lauren's admiration for military style, captured by Arthur Elgort in American Vogue, 1991.

for the lives people would like to be living as well as the lives people are living. Whether preppy or redolent of the prairie; rugged and outdoorsy or red-carpet fantasy; encompassing the soft pink taffeta gown worn by Gwyneth Paltrow to the Oscars or the mannish garb of Diane Keaton in Woody Allen's classic New York love story, *Annie Hall*, Lauren's clothes smack of authenticity. As Buck put it: "The clothes of Ralph Lauren are a form of cinema, they fulfill the private function known in movies as the back story – telling you who you are and who you were and where you come from – and the public function of demonstrating these things to other people."

With the Moscow store opening, there was a temptation for the press to re-create Lauren's own back story. Here, wrote some, drawing on Lauren's much-publicized Russian origins, was everyone's all-American boy returning to his roots, a quiet homecoming amidst all the gloss and the glamour. After all, the designer who had put the American flag so firmly on the world map of fashion was known to be fascinated by Russia; you could see it in some of his collections over the years. But while the young Lauren had indeed grown up hearing about Belarus from his father and mother, who were born in Pinsk (a part of the Soviet Union until 1991 but now in Belarus), the reality to any back story, was—as it invariably is—distinct from the romance. "It was very exciting to come to Russia," said Lauren in an interview with the *New York Times*. "There is a connection to my heritage – but where I grew from is foreign to me."

Ralph Lauren was born in New York on October 14, 1939, the youngest son of Frank and Frieda Lifshitz, who had emigrated to the city in the early twentieth century. They had met in their teens at a Russian social club, married, had three children, Thelma, Leonard, and Jerome, before Ralph came along, and they lived in Mosholu Parkway, the Bronx. Lauren's father was an accomplished artist, painting intricate murals and creating wood-effect paintwork. Surrounded by artefacts from Europe and sepia photographs of his parents' wedding, Ralph listened to a mix of Russian, Polish, and Yiddish (spoken by his parents when they didn't want their children

"A GRACEFUL LEAP OF IMAGINATION INTO THE REVIVAL OF GLAMOUR."

VOGUE

to understand them). Lauren would later draw upon a Persian lamb hat that belonged to his mother as inspiration for a Russian-themed show with Cossack tunics, greatcoats, and Bolshevik tweeds: a theme he would return to on several occasions.

Of his unremarkable upbringing, Lauren has said: "I didn't dream of a certain life, I wasn't obsessed. I was a happy middle-class Jewish kid in the Bronx." Despite growing up in the same area and at the same time as Calvin Klein (they wouldn't meet until much later in life), there was nothing about Mosholu Parkway that pointed to a career in fashion. There was, however, one small, important difference setting the young Lauren apart from his friends, which would later turn out to be the key to his future. Unusually, he had a strong sense of style, and was very much aware of what was tasteful sartorially and what wasn't. Lauren was known for his sense of dress, even designing warm-up jackets for his baseball team when he was fifteen. He would root out army surplus stock and wear safari jackets and military clothes, and loved them because: "They weren't rugged. They weren't designed. They were worn by soldiers, for real things, and that's what I loved." With his brothers he'd source tartan plaid shirts or duck-hunting jackets from gun stores. His style heroes were Cary Grant, the Duke of Windsor, and Fred Astaire: as a result he devoured movies and biographies, anything that told him more about their worlds.

He was as all-American as he could be, bar his name, and this too was eventually changed. When his elder brother Jerry decided to adopt the classless, American-sounding and, most of all, easier to spell "Lauren" in the place of their parents' surname, Lenny and Ralph quickly followed suit. After graduating from school, Lauren studied business at night and worked for Allied Stores as an assistant buyer by day. "I wanted to be an artist, but I wasn't good enough; I wanted to be a basketball player, but I wasn't tall enough," he would later recall. This being the early 1960s, he sported a Kerouac beard and an old raincoat, but while this look was considered antiestablishment, at the same time he was drawn to the classic heritage of Brooks Brothers, enjoying the atmosphere that seemed stitched into the very seams of the clothes. He would soon leave Allied Stores to work for them.

Quite what a Bronx hipster like Lauren was doing falling for Brooks Brothers' preppy styles, wasn't immediately obvious. Considered stuffy and outmoded, the button-down shirts and college sweaters seemed at once both other-worldly and all-American; a way of dressing that hadn't change since the 1940s. Lauren's keen eye was already intrigued by what he saw, even if he didn't quite know what to do with it yet. "In the Twenties," he would later say, explaining his fascination with the store. "Brooks Brothers would go sell their products to the Ivy League schools – Harvard, Princeton, Yale. They built that world, it was like a club, and kids would go to the store because that's where their fathers went. I loved the Ivy League look, the chinos with little buckles in the back, the brown and white saddle shoes, the button-down shirts. Those Oxford button-down shirts, which only came in white, pink, blue, yellow and a blue-and-white stripe, that's all. They didn't have to do any styles, year after year it was the same. I bought my first suit at Brooks Brothers for one hundred dollars, and the other clothes I wore were old army and navy stuff. When I worked there, up on the sixth floor, I'd buy stuff on the main floor, where the real things were. I'd buy one shirt and watch customers come in and order ten white shirts, shirts by the stacks. I still don't do that."

At twenty-two, after army service and stints as a glove and then a tie salesman, "I started to see that I had ideas about clothes," said Lauren. "What I imagined was a marriage of Fred Astaire and Brooks Brothers. And I'd see these ideas turn up in the stores six months later – not that anyone was copying me, but because I was on the wavelength." Before long he had spotted the gap in the market. The concept of designer menswear was growing in popularity in London with designers such as Hardy Amies, Mr Fish, and John Stephen meeting the demands of a peacock revolution, but it barely existed in the United States. Lauren turned to ties as a way of bringing a touch of modernity to an industry steeped in tradition. "I didn't know how to make a tie. I didn't know fabric. I didn't know measurements. What did I know? That I was a salesman. That I was honest. And that all I wanted was quality." He was turned down by two companies he approached before garnering support from Beau Brummel, who agreed

to back him. The twenty-eight-year old had to take care of everything from design to distribution. His brother Jerry was drafted in to help and after brainstorming English-sounding names ("Cricket" was an early option), they settled on "Polo," which spoke of tradition, class, and established wealth—"the image of the good life reflecting a style of international high society"—he would later explain to André Leon Talley in *Vogue Paris*. In 1967 Ralph Lauren was, for the first time, in business.

The ties themselves were revolutionary. They echoed a trend that had already caught on in Britain for wide ties, there known as the kipper tie, but unlike that flamboyant version, Lauren's interpretation could be worn by serious men, professionals. Polo ties were designed for men appreciating a more directional approach to fashion, yet with a nod to convention. The first to pick them up was Roland Meledandri, only his being a custom-tailoring store, they came without Lauren's label. Bloomingdale's turned him down—unless he agreed to make them narrower and sell them under their label—but not for long. Six months later they asked him back—on his terms—and even at what was considered to be the exorbitant price of $15, Bloomingdales sold out. Lauren delivered the ties himself and would call in twice a week to see how they were selling.

Lauren stood out from other tie salesmen—not only were his ties so different they necessitated a demonstration of how to tie them correctly, "plumped out so that a dimple blossomed just under the collar," but he looked unique: in tweed and combat gear or a leather aviator jacket and blue jeans, his dress sense was more like that of the actor Steve McQueen. Soon he was being asked by men if he could design shirts with collars big enough to fit these new, wider ties. They wanted suits and sportswear too. A full line of menswear was launched in 1968. "Men were wearing three-button Ivy League suits," he said. "I liked the English spirit but not the big shoulders. I made soft-shouldered jackets with wide lapels, which wasn't allowed, but it was my look. I made them in tweed and linen; the suits were what I wanted."

A mannish shirt tied at the midriff, coupled with boyfriend denims, is a versatile Lauren staple. "Knotted with jeans it's pure cowgirl," said British Vogue in 1994. Photograph by Fabrizio Ferri.

overleaf The covetable Ricky handbag (left), named after Ricky Lauren, Ralph's wife, here photographed by Raymond Meier. Clean-cut, oversize, the white shirt is given a sculptural feel (right), all the while maintaining a relaxed quality. Photographed by David Bailey for British Vogue, 1992.

By 1969 a Polo by Ralph Lauren store had opened in Bloomingdale's. A year later, Lauren won his first Coty Award, selected by members of the fashion press, in the category of highest creativity in men's fashion design. Writing in the *Columbus Dispatch* newspaper in 1970, Eleanor Lambert approved: "Lauren has never swung the axe wildly on the classic foundations. He infiltrates instead of storming, with lasting effect. His current barrier-breaker, the completely unconstructed suit, was introduced last spring in cotton madras … For some reason, the mens' industry had never produced soft suits with tasteful cut and tailoring in anything but seersucker. It was a sort of bombshell, now it's taken off across the country."

Before long, the first Polo Ralph Lauren store was opened in Rodeo Drive, Beverly Hills—the first freestanding store for an American designer. Lauren's success was based on the same guiding principle he had applied when creating his ties: "I used to take my ties home and knot them, and they were perfect," he recalled in an interview in 1982. "They represented what I stood for: quality, realness, specialness. I loved them, and everything I did from then on, I loved. Because I made what I loved, my life was there."

Stepping out: Ralph and the woman who inspired him to make his first menswear-influenced designs for women—his wife Ricky. Lauren's first tuxedo for women was deemed by some commentators "a mistake"—forty-six years on, it remains a Collection classic.

If Lauren was indeed making what he loved, his next move was to be inspired by the woman he loved—his wife, Ricky Anne Low-Beer, a blue-eyed blonde with model looks who was working part-time to help fund her way through college. The couple married in 1964. "I wanted to get her a man's jacket and shirt but she was a little girl, a size four, and no one had them," Lauren explained in later years. "So that was my first women's line, making shirts for women. I made these skinny little men's shirts with white collars, and people were buying them like candy. It was unbelievable." The shirts he made were embellished at the cuff with an embroidered logo of a man playing polo, mallet raised high in the air as the horse galloped forward. The year was 1971 and the Polo logo had just made its first outing. So too had Ralph Lauren's womenswear. The foundations of an empire had been laid.

"RALPH'S WORK HAS
BECOME SYNONYMOUS
WITH AMERICAN DESIGN AS
A BIGGER IDEA, NOT JUST
SPORTSWEAR, BECAUSE OF
ITS PURITY IN VISION."

PHILLIP LIM

"RALPH'S WORK HAS
BECOME SYNONYMOUS
WITH AMERICAN DESIGN AS
A BIGGER IDEA, NOT JUST
SPORTSWEAR, BECAUSE OF
ITS PURITY IN VISION."
PHILLIP LIM

TARTAN, TWEED, AND TAILORING

Twenty years after Lauren's first womenswear catwalk show, Joan Juliet Buck commented in American *Vogue*: "In 1971 a magazine asked: 'Will [Ralph Lauren] become America's first star designer to emerge directly from men's wear?' The answer is a resounding yes, and more: America's first star designer to turn the rest of the world on to clothes that are not clothes but little pieces of an ideal world. And not just the American of Top-Siders and western gear and Ivy League and polo shirts but the England of Father's prewar overcoat and Aunt Sibyl's cape and Ian's Fair Isle vest, all the while spewing out artefacts from those worlds with which to furnish a home or two and evolving, himself, toward a sleek and racy present that fits his favourite adjective, the word cool."

The reaction in the press to Lauren's first womenswear collection was a balance of caution and optimism. America was intrigued by a new wave of designers more in tune with a puritan aesthetic. New names such as Issey Miyake and Kenzo, were just starting out and their clean lines and ease of dressing came as timely palate cleansers for a market more used to the flair and embellishment of Yves Saint Laurent, Courrèges, and Dior. Homegrown talent like Bill Blass and Oscar de la Renta had already built names for themselves with their evening wear, but there was a definite opening on a global platform for the kind of tailored jackets and pants Lauren had been making for men for the last few years which, when tailored to fit a woman, gave her a sense of presence, confidence, and ease.

What America needed was "Pleasing Clothes" as the *New York Times* advocated in their review of the fall collections of a small group of designers. Evaluating Ralph Lauren's debut, the writer's admiration was tempered with a note of caution—Lauren should not push women too far down the path of menswear: "With all the talk about classics someone was bound to bring back the mannish tailored suit. Fortunately it was Ralph Lauren, who knows something about tailored. Mannish too, for that matter ... And now he has introduced his first woman's collection.

Helena Christensen wears a navy wool cape fastened with a gold rope clasp, over a tailored navy wool jacket with gold embroidered burgundy velvet collar and cuffs. Photographed at the Rococo Catherine Palace, Pushkin, St. Petersburg, for British Vogue, 1990, by Sante D'Orazio.

overleaf Perfectly tailored in tweed: Neil Kirk photographed this checked suit with fitted jacket and pleated pants, worn with a classic Lauren silk shirt and bouclé tie, for British Vogue, 1990.

"WITH HIS REMARKABLE TALENT FOR MINUTE OBSERVATIONS, LAUREN WAS PERFECTLY PLACED TO TAKE EXISTING STAID BASICS AND MAKE THEM BETTER."

VOGUE

He calls it sophisticated sportswear, but tailored suits would be more apt. They're in gray flannel, herringbone tweeds, classic checks. Some are worn with button-down shirts or vests. They sell for $200 to $250 and for the woman who realizes mannish tailoring can make her look more feminine, they're a neat idea. As for the tuxedos for women, they're a mistake." A "mistake" which the Collection label today still sells – at $3500 a piece.

It is hard today to appreciate the impact the show made on women's closets. As Lisa Armstrong would later write in British *Vogue*: "Internationally there was no Gap to disseminate American style. No Calvin Klein underwear. No designer jeans. Nothing that would give the States a branded identity. With his remarkable talent for minute observations, Lauren was perfectly placed to take existing staid basics and make them better ... The States was more than ready to feed on an idealised vision of itself." Fashion writer and historian Colin McDowell goes so far as to liken Lauren to an American Coco Chanel with her informal style and easy-to-wear Chanel suits: "What Ralph Lauren proposed was not unique. Chanel had understood the appeal of the dégagé approach to dress."

While such accolades are well deserved, Lauren would be the first to admit he was taken by surprise by the success that followed. "It wasn't like I did this amazing collection in Paris and everyone just got up and applauded and said, 'You're marvellous!'" he would later recall. "I would have wished that happened to me when I first started ... I didn't know anything about the women's business. I just went and had the clothes made in a men's factory. I bought the factory later. The tailors there laughed at me ... I said, 'I want this suit for my wife; take this suit, scale it down.' I shortened the jackets, made them slim, with skinny arms. They fitted some women and others couldn't get into them. They were limited to flat-chested girls. I was aiming at women like Ricky, and models. It became an in thing."

"HE HAS INFORMED A CERTAIN WAY OF DRESSING THAT I THINK RESONATES WITH ALL OF US ... AND HAS BECOME A PART OF THE VERNACULAR OF AMERICAN DESIGN."

PHILLIP LIM

And yet in spite of his candor and "it-just-sorta-happened" modesty, it was, in its own way, revolutionary. When actress Candice Bergen was photographed for American *Vogue* in head-to-toe Ralph Lauren, playing with a dog on the beach, the caption tellingly described the clothes as "the nothing-fashion of all time." The rules of dressing had changed. *Vogue* readers wanted "the easy glamour of the casual, sportswear attitude of dressing; of hatlessness and hair blowing; of fresh, unpretentious, easy good looks … the classic image of American style we've all grown up with."

But this time, it was different. There was nothing hit and miss about what Lauren was offering. Separates had to work together; the type of "whipped-cream sportswear with chiffon scarves floating everywhere" that had been offered up to now was to be abandoned in favor of Lauren's trimmer lines: "nothing is floating around or cluttering up or weighting down" wrote American *Vogue* in 1976. A jacket could be worn like a shirt; a coat could be a raincoat; the overall effect was of pared down, weightless dressing, with "a narrow little ribbon belt that slips through rings" replacing anything as bohemian as a chiffon scarf tied around the waist. How could a suit be at the same time "sportswear"? asked the same magazine six months later. The season's hacking suit was the answer, "not what a suit used to be, but what it can be now, the way Ralph Lauren does it. The zip-front jacket and fly-front trouser [pant] skirt in lightest chamois-color brushed cotton gabardine—neat as a pin and easy as jeans."

Whole articles were devoted to this new way of dressing. "Learn from a man … what you can do with a suit" was the title of one, which extolled the virtues of Ralph Lauren's "perfect wool plaid hacking jacket and skirt" as being the kind of suit you can pull apart and put together six different ways for six days running without looking as though you're running out of steam. Texture was important—a bird's eye Harris Tweed, a Donegal tweed, a herringbone, a plaided flannel, a Shetland tweed, the kind of fabric that didn't feel flat to the touch—was key to the look. Classic menswear patterns on knits were

previous pages An All-American girl all in Ralph Lauren: Candice Bergen wearing a casual white sweater and pants, laughing on the beach, is the epitome of Lauren's lifestyle approach to fashion, "the nothing-fashion of all time" according to American Vogue in 1973. Photograph by Melvin Sokolsky.

encouraged for their versatility especially if the colors were soft and blended well with each other.

Above everything else, the cut could make or break the look, something which Lauren had by now adjusted and perfected for his female customers, supported by a team that included his business partner Peter Strom, his brothers Lenny and Jerry, and on the design side ex-*Daily News Record* journalist Buffy Birrittella and Sal Cesarini, a sketcher and tailor. The design process would start by examining a pair of men's pants, noting how the details could be incorporated into a woman's skirt. American *Vogue* advised its readers: "A quarter-inch too much length in the jacket, it's wrong over skirts. A quarter-inch too short, it's funny over pants. You want a length that stops where your leg starts. And you want a quick narrow fit from the shoulder down; not nipped at the waist, not tight anywhere – like a man's sports jacket, it should be able to take heavy sweaters as well as cotton shirts."

The classic women's pant suit would remain a mainstay of Ralph Lauren's collections; so too would the fastidiousness with which it was made. Over the years, keeping it fresh and desirable would become something of an obsession. Writing in American *Vogue* in 1996, Mary Tannen described the fitting process in the run up to Lauren's fall/winter show with his by now massively expanded team. Lauren would begin with one pant suit from his men's line and cut it down for a woman, using the thirteen patternmakers, eight tailors, and seven dressmakers in his atelier to make prototypes of the designs. Watching him work, she observed, "The lapel is pinned narrower, the arms slimmed, the body brought in. The trousers [pants] are shortened so that instead of breaking over the shoes they end right above. Everyone stands around Schafer [Alexandra Schafer, the model], looking in the mirror at the suit. The altered measurements are carefully entered into a notebook that has a section for every garment. Polaroids document the changes. A sketcher begins drawing the way it looks now." She continued, "In the days to come, he will fall in and out of love with the suit. It will almost not make it into the show, but in an inspired flash, he will add a black shirt and tie and tuck a pink silk hankie into the pocket.

"WHEN I STARTED 40 YEARS AGO, I MADE ALL THE THINGS I COULDN'T FIND."

RALPH LAUREN

As Lauren's reputation grew, American Vogue pictured him on a horse, surrounded by models wearing his lifestyle-friendly looks. Photographed by Oliviero Toscani in 1977.

overleaf Robert Redford, as Jay Gatsby, is the perfect vehicle for Lauren's sharp suiting, worn in the 1974 movie version of The Great Gatsby.

"WHEN I STARTED 40 YEARS AGO, I MADE ALL THE THINGS I COULDN'T FIND."

RALPH LAUREN

As Lauren's reputation grew, American Vogue pictured him on a horse, surrounded by models wearing his lifestyle-friendly looks. Photographed by Oliviero Toscani in 1977.

overleaf Robert Redford, as Jay Gatsby, is the perfect vehicle for Lauren's sharp suiting, worn in the 1974 movie version of The Great Gatsby.

"I WAS DOING GATSBY LONG BEFORE THE GREAT GATSBY CAME OUT."

RALPH LAUREN

When Sarah O'Hare, with her cropped copperish hair, takes it down the runway, the suit will be what everyone wants to own."

By 1977 what had started out as a few clothes for Ricky Lauren had taken off into a full-scale closet. American *Vogue* ran a double-page spread of the designer sitting on a horse, surrounded by ten models, male and female, clad in various looks fit for work, home, and evening, all drawing on his, by now, well-established principles of easy dressing. A year prior to this, he had received his second Coty Award for womenswear and a Coty Hall of Fame Award for menswear, the first designer to win both men's and women's categories in the same year.

Aside from the fashion pundits, Lauren had another, unexpected ally. His rapid rise was helped in no small part by his being able to reach millions of Americans via an unexpected source: Hollywood. In March 1973 the late costume designer Theoni Aldredge was appointed to design the clothes for *The Great Gatsby*, the movie—starring Robert Redford and Mia Farrow—of the great American novel by F. Scott Fitzgerald, with its American Dream storyline pitting the new-money Jay Gatsby against the old-money East Egg social set of Daisy Buchanan. Long before the movie was even shooting, department stores were promoting Gatsby-inspired menswear; such was the excitement. Ralph Lauren's contemporary take on tradition that ran through all his menswear collections was an obvious fit for this 1970s meets 1920s visualization. "I was doing Gatsby long before *The Great Gatsby* came out," he would later recall. "That's what I did. It was glamorous. When people couldn't understand what my clothes were about I talked about Gatsby—it was the era of the jackets with belted backs, of flannel suits."

Aldredge commissioned Lauren to work on the project, dressing not only the leading actors but all the extras too. He immediately applied himself to creating a look that had the spirit of the 1920s but yet would appeal to a modern audience. "The trick is not to look like Polo but the period," Lauren told *GQ* magazine in 1974. "In 1925, shirts were cut fuller and collars were shorter and not

previous pages *Lauren provided the closet for Diane Keaton and Woody Allen, in the movie* Annie Hall *(1977). He based Annie's closet on Diane Keaton's own eclectic style.*

spread so wide and they took a smaller, knotted, unlined tie." Lauren's closet did wonders for the movie and though Aldredge would openly accuse Lauren of attempting to take all the credit (the press went into overdrive, lapping up Lauren's designs and exaggerating his own "rags-to-riches" story, comparing it with that of the protagonist, Jay Gatsby), his work undoubtedly contributed to her receiving an Academy Award for costume design. For Lauren there were bigger prizes than gold statuettes. As Jeffrey Trachtenberg wrote, "It also did wonders for his career. For despite the Coty Awards, the store on Rodeo Drive, and the support from Bloomingdale's, the name Ralph Lauren was little known to the general public. Now he was getting national exposure."

Bagging one all-American classic movie would suffice for some, but Lauren was so much in tune with the zeitgeist that he became involved in a second great movie of the decade. Woody Allen's *Annie Hall* (1977), starring Allen himself and Diane Keaton. While again he wasn't the official costume designer, although he did supply clothes for the leads, all the Lauren trademarks were nonetheless present—"the mixes of tweed and plaid, the sepia touch of a little tie or a thread along the edge of the collar that was a connotation of the past and the big battered no-color hat" wrote Buck in American *Vogue*. Keaton and Allen had already been fans of his clothes for some time. "Annie's style was Diane's style – very eclectic," explained Lauren. "Oversized jackets and vests, floppy men's hats and cowboy boots. We shared a sensibility, but she had a style that was all her own. Annie Hall was pure Diane Keaton." The impact of the movie was again, huge.

"Personal style is about having a sense of yourself
and what you believe in."

RALPH LAUREN

"After we women saw *Annie Hall*, in which Diane Keaton wore his long skirts, shirts, vests and a man's jacket over everything, a bulky, endearing, nostalgic but anarchic waif, we suddenly began to borrow our mens' jackets and wear them with the sleeves rolled up," wrote Buck. "[It] all coalesced on *Annie Hall* and suggested a truly new and independent way of dressing. Lauren's androgyny was not the sleek perfection of Yves Saint Laurent nor the as-yet-unborn professional style of Armani; it was tender, personal, and original. In the film it showed Annie Hall's eccentricity, her sexual hesitancy, her wish to be invincible and invisible. In real life it showed an alliance of practicality and nostalgia, and the wearing of an oversize tweed jacket still states a refusal of passing fads in preference of the older values, for what lasts."

While Lauren's collections evolved into closet staples which could be reworked according to the season—the gamekeeper jackets, the elongated sweater, the polo shirt, the long, tight T-shirts, and the tuxedo—at their core was this preference for older values. Lauren's style heroines were women such as Katharine Hepburn, Grace Kelly, Lauren Bacall, and Audrey Hepburn, women who exuded a relaxed confidence. His clothes weren't following fashion; they spoke of integrity and quality. "It's for someone who doesn't want to look like she's trying too hard," said Birrittella. "She's wearing the clothes, the clothes aren't wearing her. She's very confident and so nothing is forced or gimmicky or costumey. So right away at the beginning a philosophy evolved, even if the reference was menswear."

"Rekindling that masculine style with a strong feminine curve," said American Vogue *of Christy Turlington joining the ranks of the Arduduy Male Voice Choir in a Ralph Lauren tailcoat, vest, and silk shirt, and captured by Arthur Elgort in 1992.*

Lauren would return to his contemporary take on traditional tailoring in time, eventually honing it into a more British style in the early 1980s, presenting an American view of aristocratic dressing. Once again, he looked for the genuine article: cloth that came from wool mills in the West Country or Yorkshire, tweed from Scotland. "I don't know exactly how I got involved with the whole English thing but I did and it was very important to me but, whatever it was, I saw it entirely through American eyes," he later explained. Here were tweed jackets, skirts, Aran sweaters, that weren't just replicas. They were contemporary classics, with a life of their own. How would they differ

from the real McCoy? As partner Peter Strom elaborated in American *Vogue* in 1982, "Our Shetland sweater sells for more than anybody else's because it was conceived by Ralph to have a seamless shoulder, a seamless body, and a hand-linked neck. It took us a year just to get the weight right. We made two trips to Scotland to finalize the manufacturing standards, only to learn they couldn't do it without seams. Nobody said, 'Ralph, you've got to have seams.' We went to Hong Kong and got someone in the business to make it for us."

The English look also served a very practical purpose: it was a way to take the mannish appeal of Lauren's earlier designs forward while staying true to the brand's signature tailoring: to give a wistful, sometimes romantic feel without becoming too girlish or losing the traditional values that spoke volumes to Lauren's audience. In *Vogue*, Buck described the clothes as having "a great deal of activity at the neck: a paisley ascot [tie] in a bow over a lace jabot under a tweed jacket, or a high-necked shirt, an ascot, a hand-crocheted waistcoat [vest] with a watch chain. There are stocks, those extraordinarily long white ties that you wind around your neck eight or nine times when you wear your hunting pink." All were derived from existing classic Lauren outfits: long skirts, jodhpurs, pin-striped suits, and vests.

Mario Testino imagines a day at the races for model Jasmine Guinness with an entourage of suitably aristocratic young guns, British Vogue *2004.*

How did the British feel about their culture being packaged so? Joan Burstein, of Brown's, who with her husband Sidney opened the first Ralph Lauren store in Bond Street (now a Ralph Lauren childrenswear store) was quoted as saying: "The British like it because it is also the ambiance they would like to be part of. It's what they think the London society scene looks like, how those people dress and put their things together. It's all part of an image. Why hasn't Jaeger done it, or Liberty of London? They can't. They don't have the business sense, the mentality." Perhaps there was an even simpler answer, as Armstrong wrote in British *Vogue*: "When (Lauren) first visited England at the end of the Sixties, he was shocked that the men weren't in bowler hats and you couldn't buy a Fair Isle jumper [sweater] that didn't feel like a loofah when you wore it. So he made his own." The British could now look British, but more comfortably so.

"I WAS INFLUENCED BY BRITISH FASHION, BUT NOT [JUST] FASHION: BRITISH PEOPLE."

RALPH LAUREN

The white collar overlaid on black has become something of a signature for Lauren. Here the collar and cuffs for the long wool crepe dress on the right are detachable; the finely fitted chalk-stripe jacket on the left, worn over a long pleated gray wool crepe skirt is yet another example of Lauren's mannish style given a feminine touch. Photographed by Patrick Demarchelier for British Vogue, 1992.

previous page Venetia Scott photographs a Highland plaid lady's redingote in Scotland, as modeled by Kamila Filipcikova for British Vogue, 2008. The themes of tartan, tweed, and tailoring have been constantly updated by Ralph Lauren since his first collection was sent down the catwalk in 1971.

"THE COURAGE TO ALWAYS
BE HIMSELF IS ONE OF THE
QUALITIES I MOST ADMIRE IN
HIM. ANYTHING HE DOES HAS
THE DNA OF HIS STYLE."

VALENTINO

THE
DREAMCATCHER

"I'm not an artist working alone in his studio, designing the perfect armhole," Lauren once said. "I was the guy looking at the magazines and movies, saying 'Wow, that's where I'd like to be.' The way I see it, you've got to paint the environment. It's not just the car, it's where you're going in that car. I'm trying to paint a wonderful world, a life that makes you feel good. Maybe I'm redefining a life we lost. That's my movie. What's yours?" If Lauren's clothes were movies, Western wear was about to be his great American blockbuster, capturing the frontier spirit, the cowboys sitting around the campfire, the traditions of the Native Americans, all of which were held dear by an entire nation. It would be a happily-ever-after leitmotif he would return to in the same way you could rewatch a classic cowboy movie, only reworked around certain staples, like the concho belt (a leather belt embellished with burnished metal emblems) and the Navajo jacket. As it evolved it would at times be bolder, as with his fringed pants and jackets; or prettier, as with the lace petticoats, but he would always stay on the right side of classic, rather than stray into the realms of caricature.

Model Tatjana Patitz shows off a utilitarian side to Western wear, boyish yet feminine when styled with a floral cotton shirt. The cotton canvas coat is typical of the workwear aesthetic of Lauren's Roughwear line. Photographed by Arthur Elgort for American Vogue, 1989.

In 1978, while New York was getting on down to the Bee Gees' "Saturday Night Fever," the models who stepped out on Lauren's fall/winter catwalk show were accompanied by Gene Autry's gently lilting Western classic, "Back in the Saddle Again." Hidden in the lyrics is the line, "I go my way"—apt for Lauren, whose brave move to go west, taking a left turn away from his popular mannish styles was to prove a surefire hit, appealing to urban cowboys everywhere. "Western is Lauren's big statement for fall '78, but it's very much his own way with the West: fringed buckskin, chamois, or leather jackets; flounced prairie skirts with tweed jackets; shearling vests," wrote Kathleen Madden in American *Vogue*. "Un-hokey pieces that can slip into – not rupture – a woman's wardrobe [closet]." The finale of the show featured a disco. Beverly Johnson appeared in a long red mink coat with a concho belt and high gold cowboy boots to a backdrop of flashing lights.

Exquisitely ethereal, Ralph Lauren's lace and crochet gowns portray a fantasy of Americana meets Edwardiana, captured by Mario Testino for American Vogue, 2011, which called them "the new romantics."

The appeal was instantaneous. Here was a look that was so much a part of the American psyche it was a wonder no one had pulled it together before. "It has a pioneer look." Lauren said at the time. "It has an earthiness. It has realness. It's not costumey. That's what I relate to." He'd been a fan ever since he was a boy, and would regularly turn up at black-tie events wearing a Western-style tie with a formal dinner jacket. "The Western thing for the woman. I think is very much the same as it is for the man: wearing things that have a classic integrity to them that are not fashion per se. but that are individual. They are romantic in that they represent a world that we've all grown up with and love, whether it be through the movies or our dreams. You know. Western clothes could be dumb. They could be corny. They could be glossy. I sense a romanticism, and I express this in texture, in the quality, the spirit I believe in. My Western clothes look like me, they don't look like Roy Rogers."

The Old West was now the stuff that dreams were made of, with urban cowboys popping up everywhere. "New York has become something of a cowboy town." wrote *The Times*. "Men whose idea of a canyon is the space between two rows of skyscrapers take the air in full regalia – 10-gallon hat. yoked shirt. embroidered denim jacket, hand-tooled belt, jeans and boots. And the women beside them wreathe their throats in bandannas. wear ankle-length skirts fit for a hoedown and – faced with inclement weather – don hats and ponchos worthy of the crew of a cattle drive."

The fringed detail of Western wear, brought by Ralph Lauren to the urban lifestyle, made city cowboys of us all. Tatjana Patitz, in a soft suede coat, stops for a refuel, photographed by Arthur Elgort for American Vogue, 1989.

Lauren's love of the West would endure. In 1980, he took Ricky and their children to New Mexico for a vacation which would provide the inspiration for his Santa Fe collection the following year. While Calvin Klein had also visited New Mexico that year and drawn on it for his collection. Lauren's designs were a world away from Klein's muted palette. Chamois skirts, turquoise hoop earrings. Navajo Fair-Isle sweaters with strong patterns and bright colors. mixed in ways not seen by the world's fashion press before, looked fresh and exciting, especially when styled over his white cotton blouses, long prairie skirts, and full white petticoats.

Overnight, Ralph Lauren made the concho belt
a collector's item. "It's a classic – like a good
watch you keep forever." Above, it ties together a
Native-American-patterned wool turtleneck and
suede dirndl skirt. Photographed for American
Vogue, 1981, by Marco Glaviano.
Over the years Lauren's signature fringing has
evolved, but its roots remain firmly entrenched
in the romance of the Old West. Freja Beha
Erichsen demonstrates the modernity of
the look, (right) photographed by Patrick
Demarchelier for British Vogue, 2011.

"I've always had a sense of the many things in this country that were interesting, and Americana was very appealing to me," he explained. "With the Indian blankets, I happen to like the colors, the fade, the warm materials." The blankets would eventually lead to sweaters and would also be incorporated in his home collections.

Overnight, concho belts—made from the silver pieces developed by the Navajos and then adapted by the Pueblo tribe of New Mexico—became collector's items. Lauren teamed them with bare midriffs and long rickrack skirts for his resort collection. "The concho [belt] is a classic – like a good watch you keep forever – a wonderful investment and I believe in that kind of product. It looks great – whether you wear it with corduroys or thin summer cottons. It's the antique of the future."

The look was much copied by others. Lauren deliberately created his following collections as softer, less literal interpretations; he cites his fall 1982 show as being one of his great collections, with its gentle, Folk-Art feel and pioneer influence. He also focused on the more workwear aspects of the West, as reflected in the 1989 American *Vogue* shoot by photographer Arthur Elgort. To critics who accused him of plundering tradition, he had this answer: "I was inspired by the West, by things no longer here that I wanted to see again. I couldn't buy a great Western shirt anywhere. Everything was polyester." Meanwhile, his nod to Americana was more than appreciated by the associated crafts and design industries it breathed a new energy into. In 1988 the American Folk Art Museum honored Lauren with an award for Pioneering Excellence in American style. That same year, Deborah Turbeville photographed Faye Dunaway wearing Ralph Lauren in Santa Fe. The caption described the scene accordingly: "A woman alone on a big ranch, terribly isolated on a perfectly beautiful day. At one with nature but subtly menaced by the stillness." The Western look captured the imaginations of all.

Daria Werbowy in a floral silk georgette tiered dress puts a spin on the classic Edwardiana fantasy. Photographed by Patrick Demarchelier, for British Vogue, 2008.

overleaf Lauren has an enduring love for Native American geometric patterns, interpreted here in a long Navaho-print wool coat, modeled by Tatjana Patitz and photographed for American Vogue by Arthur Elgort in 1989.

"'I WAS INSPIRED BY THE SPIRIT OF THE RUGGED WEST, THE ROMANCE OF THE PRAIRIE, AND HOW A MODERN, STYLISH WOMAN WOULD WEAR IT."

RALPH LAUREN

Life on the Prairie, and the beauty of Navajo Fair-Isle sweaters mixed with patterned coats and dirndl skirts, captured the essence of Americana and showcased it to the world. Photographed by Bruce Weber, 1982, for British Vogue.

overleaf *Ralph Lauren, with campaign girl Clotilde wearing a patchwork jacket. One of the first designers to recognize the importance of telling a story through his advertising, he worked with a "family" of models to create a narrative that allowed him to sell his clothes as total looks. Photograph by Eric Boman for Vogue Paris, 1982.*

It was an association that was mutually beneficial, with Weber likening his relationship with Lauren in the early days as being like that of an adopted son receiving an expensive college education, as he was dispatched around the world to gather ideas. "Ralph would send me to Paris to take pictures and explore the French underground and nightlife," he said, years later, in *Vogue Paris*. "He also sent me to London to photograph these aristocrats he knew through books and movies, people who attended elegant men's clubs, went to dinner dances at the Connaught and Claridge's or lived discreetly in Mayfair mansions containing more dogs than could be counted on both hands."

With Weber, but sometimes with other A-lister photographers such as Sheila Metzner, Lauren rolled out a series of detailed campaigns that would sometimes run to twenty pages. All were propped down to the tiniest characteristic, from exactly how worn the carpet should be to the number of walking sticks positioned in the hallway. His shoots were as alive as movie sets with an all important narrative and a cast of men, women, children, and animals. Most of all, they allowed Lauren to record his clothes as total looks, to set them in an atmosphere that conveyed his particular vision; in so doing, he created the concept of clothes as lifestyle.

Nothing was too much trouble; compromise was not an option. One such difficult-to-execute and yet, as a result, highly impactful campaign was Lauren's Safari shoot of 1984, a series of photos which appeared—somewhat presciently—before *Out of Africa* was made into a movie. The look was, in Lauren's words, all about "the contrast of sturdy khakis, jodhpurs, and camp shirts against the elegance of pearls and romantic lace blouses, and cream linen suits worn with dusty riding boots." Lauren had never been to Africa, and Weber was reluctant to shoot there, having found it difficult on location there in the 1970s. Perhaps Hawaii could be a stand-in? Lauren's team found a private ranch complete with African trees and vast landscapes; the only thing missing was the animals. Protracted negotiations with officials about how best to import lion cubs, and possibly a zebra, resulted in a list of conditions which included strict animal quarantine and the presence of a state official while they were shooting. It had long been the practice of Lauren and his staff to collect objects that would inspire—for the Western wear collections they had been accumulating vintage pieces for years, from concho belts to petticoats to patchwork quilts to help them put together their Western-themed idyll. But no one had thought they might need to collect lion cubs. Lauren wasn't prepared to accept anything short of the real thing.

Birrittella picks up the story: "Lions only breeding at a certain point, all the cubs were already too big to be safely handled," she explained. A friend came to the rescue: he knew the actress Tippi Hedren who had a ranch in California where she raised lions. "She let us have three lion cubs and one ten-month-old lion which was almost full-grown. But I still needed that zebra!" She found one, only to discover that the zebra would need to fly in a cargo plane, at a cost of $22,000. After much bargaining, Pan Am brought the price down. Builders, carpenters, and upholsterers were then dispatched to create the set. "As if nothing had happened," said Weber, in a later interview, "we saw on location a rather grumpy zebra and several lion cubs!"

A resounding success, a perfume was launched on the back of the collection, called Safari, only this time the TV commercial was

Reviving the era of glamorous travel: Andie MacDowell impeccably dressed in a raw silk jacket and linen culottes, photographed by Albert Watson for British Vogue, 1982.

filmed by Les Goldberg in East Africa, using Ernest Hemingway's *The Snows of Kilimanjaro* and Isak Dinesen's 1937 memoir *Out of Africa* as the inspiration, and featuring the model Kim Nye. The East Africa shoot was no less a labor of love, with a small village of over 50 tents erected for the crew; props, furnishings, and extras flown in, and Maasai warriors hired as guards. The perfume would go on to become a classic, with the cut-crystal bottle, sealed with a gold cover, now a part of the permanent collection of the Cooper-Hewitt National Design Museum in New York.

Lauren was a born story-maker, and the life of the British upper classes was as rich in narratives as the great plains of Africa or the prairies of the Midwest. His tailored tweeds and knitted separates had already underscored several of his collections; now it was their turn to be brought into the limelight with a sprinkle of the Lauren-Weber magic. In 1984 another elaborate shoot took place, this time at Cliveden for Lauren's English collection. Twenty people flew over from the States, and a cast and crew of forty-four in total settled in at the stately home in Berkshire formerly owned by the Astor family. Exactly the right type of dog was needed—be they spaniels, Labradors, setters, fox terriers, Scotties, Jack Russells, Dalmatians, Yorkies, Bedlingtons, collies, or Pomeranians. "Ralph has always agreed when I wanted lots of dogs and children to pose alongside girls dressed in sumptuous evening dresses and men in impeccably-cut suits," remembered Weber. The models in this and subsequent campaigns were never just models; they appeared as characters fit for *Downton Abbey* or, even, the series screening on American television at the time, *Brideshead Revisited*. They never smiled, but would stand outside grand stately homes, all the while conveying a sense of wild beauty through their good genes.

The day before the memorable Cliveden shoot, model Saffron Aldridge was cast as an extra for an aristocratic-looking party scene shot by Weber at London's Park Lane Hotel. At the end of the day, Weber selected three of the extras to join him at Cliveden. Aldridge was disappointed not to be among them.

"Wish now for Ralph Lauren's molten-gold-sequinned genie pants," said Vogue *in 2009, pairing them for travel with a golden cotton shirt. Photograph by Mario Testino.*

A silk and linen bustier dress becomes the perfect ensemble for washing down an elephant. In the backwaters of Kerala, Daria Werbowy sets to work for Patrick Demarchelier and British Vogue, 2009.

previous pages With incredible attention to detail, Ralph Lauren's team of set designers created a highly impactful Safari campaign, with "on location, a rather grumpy zebra and several lion cubs!" according to Bruce Weber, a principal campaign photographer for several years.

overleaf A white linen coat and viscose-gabardine palazzo pants afford an effortless elegance in a desert setting. Photographed by Mikael Jansson for British Vogue, 1993.

"A WORLD THAT WE'VE ALL GROWN UP WITH AND LOVE, WHETHER ... THROUGH THE MOVIES OR OUR DREAMS."

RALPH LAUREN

Three months later, after the movie had been processed and edited, Aldridge's agent received a call from Lauren. He'd spotted her in the background of the Park Lane shoot, slightly blurred and asked, "Who's that girl?'" The first British model to sign a contract with an American designer, committing her to appear in both editorial and advertising exclusively in Ralph Lauren's clothes for the next few years, she remembers the atmosphere on the shoots: "You were presented an amazing environment, full of beautiful houses, beautiful cushions, beautiful everything, from the roses in vases to the tablecloths."

No expense was spared. "You'd fly to California and have a sunning day. Then there was the prepping day. Then you'd shoot for five days solid. It was just an incredible synchronicity that I'm not sure you'd find in fashion shoots now."

Model Saffron Aldridge, one of Lauren's campaign girls, presents the archetypal English aristocratic look. "He created a family, and as he continued to use the same people season after season, the customer felt like they knew you," she said.

The campaigns were sometimes criticized for being alienating but if so, it was an alienation that fired up the imagination and inspired dreams. Lauren's idealized worlds were invariably better than the real thing. Turning his attention to that next bastion of the Establishment, the WASP (White Anglo-Saxon Protestant)—the coterie of blue-bloods and bankers that inhabited the Hamptons and the upper echelons of Manhattan—he spotted something that was sartorially endearing: an appeal that was founded on, in his own words, "the oldness, the custom mood of navy blazers, school crests, flannels and saddle shoes." Aside from Brooks Brothers, who supplied blazers, button-down shirts, and deck shoes as regularly as a school-uniform outfitters, the rest of the world had chosen to ignore this segment of Americana. Although WASPs might have money, money didn't necessarily buy anyone style. As Paul Rudnick wryly observed in American *Vogue*, "Why would anyone want to be a WASP? Yes, you would have unlimited access to power and funds but who wants to rule the universe in penny loafers and a belt embroidered with tiny whales? Real WASP ladies go for searing hot pinks and the most Day-Glo Lilly Pullitzer florals teamed with high-gloss black patent-leather slingbacks. Real WASP men are seldom discovered sipping brandy in steel-gray cardigans and mossy corduroys.

"The blue bloods of Newport gathered on a summer evening ... the rustle of ink-black taffeta, the tinkling of jewels filled the air," wrote American Vogue in 2002, describing Mario Testino's High-Society-inspired homage to Ralph Lauren's glamorous eveningwear. Pictured are a black long-sleeved V-neck long dress and an ivory silk corset gown with black satin sash.

They're big on pimiento-toned chinos topped with jolly 'patchwork' crewnecks or ski sweaters knitted with prancing reindeer and the silhouettes of martini glasses."

Lauren—and to a degree Woody Allen, in their very different ways—turned the Hamptons set into something worthy of a fashion plate, and in so doing created the look that would become known as "preppy." Not having attended the cliquey Ivy League colleges himself, Lauren would pore over the old yearbooks of Princeton, Harvard, and Yale, and was gifted with an outsider's eye that meant he could adapt the image of the collegians without being bound by it. Rudnick's article was accompanied by nine looks of lovingly photographed fantasy-WASP clothes, from a whole roster of designers including Oscar de la Renta, Calvin Klein, DKNY, and Lauren, the point being that American style was here to stay, finally, whether it was WASP or not. What Lauren's campaigns would tap into, with their cast of persuasive characters "forever lounging over tennis courts and polo fields, cashmere sweaters thrown over their shoulders, living vicariously for the hard-working professional who can afford the clothes," as writer Georgina Howell would describe them, was the self-assurance and elegance a certain way of dressing—upper-class American dressing—could give you. It couldn't have been more timely—this being the Eighties, conservatism, tradition, and stability were values that appealed.

Ready to ride: the appeal of equestrian clothes was not just about Lauren's love of horses and riding; rather it reflected the sense of self-assurance and elegance that a certain way of dressing could imbue its wearer. Photographed by Alex Chatelain for British Vogue, 1985.

Creating worlds that had a resonance beyond mere clothes was something that was not just confined to the commercials and campaigns synonymous with the Ralph Lauren name. Within the stores, whether stand-alone or stores within department stores, as soon as they set a foot through the door customers felt that they were coming home. Lauren had always been adept at enhancing the presentation of his designs. For his very first tie display at Bloomingdales, Lauren had insisted on separate cabinets and he had a habit of picking up things here and there that would set off the clothes to their best advantage—a pile of antiqued leather books, a comfy leather library

chair, a riding crop, or a vintage patchwork quilt; things which added value and atmosphere.

He had been a visitor to London since the late Sixties, where he had enjoyed exploring the antiques markets and tailors' stores of Savile Row and Jermyn Street, occasionally accompanied by colleagues or his former creative director for Europe, Ann Boyd. His Creative Services team, well briefed and well versed in the Ralph Lauren look, were trained to scour the world's auction rooms looking for artefacts that might become cherished props in Lauren's stores. An apocryphal tale describes the Lauren creative team descending on Gray's Antique Market in London, buying up almost all the contents of a single stall before moving on to the next one and doing the same.

This was just as well, because they would have a lot of space to fill. In 1986 Lauren opened his flagship store in the Rhinelander Mansion on Madison Avenue and 72nd street. Built by New York architects Kimball and Thompson in the 1890s and based on the chateaux of the Loire Valley, it had fallen into disrepair, and Lauren set about restoring the building's opulence and grandeur. Some $30 million and several years later, the parquet floors, mahogany paneling, a grand central staircase, and renovated wooden elevators returned a sense of glory to the five-store, 20,000-square-foot (1,850-square-meter) store. Before long it was filled with the kind of props a movie set design team could only dream of. Victorian oil paintings, armchairs, mahogany tables, horn photograph frames, and cut-glass decanters gave the store a lived-in feeling which was constantly updated according to the new collections of clothes and homewares that were stocked each season.

As Lisa Armstrong wrote in British *Vogue*: "For such a well-briefed team, creating settings for the Rhinelander is a cinch. It is constantly re-dressed like a lovingly tended doll's house. A self-contained world is diligently created for each season's range; the weekend wear is surrounded by old cricket bats and ancient looking picnic hampers; on the ground floor, the ties are laid out on polished wooden counters next to huge blue and white vases of flowers.

Who's that girl? Often Lauren's clothes hinted at fantasy characters, women who traversed the globe, eternally elegant, and living the dream. Here a white suit and beret seems de rigueur for sightseeing in Venice, as photographed by Barry Lategan for British Vogue, 1983.

On the top floors, the Ralph Lauren Home Collection, where cotton drill cushion covers sell for $100 and Irish linen sheets blow out of the store for $400, there's currently a Santa Fe room, a Moroccan one and a Nice one." That same year the Paris flagship opened, equipped in the same luxurious style of its sister stores in London and New York.

Within the store, there was plenty of space for the homewares collection Lauren had first revealed in 1983. It was only natural that homewares would increasingly reflect Lauren's own lifestyle, which by now included several houses each with a distinct Ralph Lauren style. Divided into five categories, "Jamaica," "New England," "Thoroughbred," "Log Cabin," and "Color," which reflected the homes he now owned in Jamaica, Bedford, Montauk, Colorado, and Manhattan, there was something for everyone, from good-quality cotton sheets, supersoft towels to some of those money-can't-buy props, including a large wing chair upholstered in brown alligator that now could be bought, albeit at a price—$175,000. Often the homewares collections mirrored the hallmarks of his catwalk shows. Like the Santa Fe look? Treat yourself to some handworked concho silverware. Fancy a weekend lunch at the Country Club? Cashmere cable-knit blankets should help you envisage it, or why not try a button-down Oxford-cloth pillowcase?

"The thing is," said Ricky in an interview in 2012, "everything that Ralph does is to do with something he might need." The things the Lauren family needed mirrored the things customers would want to buy. Visiting the Laurens' home in Montauk, Fiona Golfar observed, "the furniture is bamboo with crisp white cushions and a comfortable, deep, white sofa [which] lines the far end of the room. Rattan baskets and wickerwork accessories are everywhere (there is even a wicker-clad bicycle in the entrance hall) and a low coffee table is covered in books, candles and flowers." In Jamaica, there was Round Hill, with its billowing drapes, mosquito netting, grass rugs, fancy chandeliers, and mahogany paneling for the backdrop to any Ralph Lauren runway show. His house in Bedford, set on 250 gently undulating acres and equipped with expansive antiqued sofas and paisley and zebra rugs, had a more English feel to it than his ranch in Colorado or the minimalist Manhattan duplex with its panoramic views of Central Park.

As Joan Juliet Buck put it in *Vogue* in 1992. "The home collections are even stronger than the ads in conveying a life, as if the person had just left the room so that you could pore over his things, trespass, and then own his essence. Even in Lauren's department-store shops there were always things around that couldn't be bought: old suitcases, riding boots, hatboxes, suchlike. When he started the home collections in 1983 it was with a flourish: the ads showed high-style rooms in which sleigh beds were heaped with linens in manifold shapes and patterns that could be bought, whereas the antique props could not."

overleaf "The homewares collection came out of needing things for our home." Ricky Lauren describes the motivation for Lauren's first forays into interiors. Photographed by Eric Boman for British Vogue, 1994.

Such luxurious necessities aside, what would make Ralph Lauren's sheets different from anybody else's? asked American *Vogue*. "The difference is you'll want to buy them." replied Lauren. "I didn't go into this to do sheets. I love homes and the things that go into them, and once I saw that I couldn't find some of the things I wanted, I was hooked." As was everyone. When his European Creative Director at the time, Ann Boyd, dressed Harvey Nichols' windows in London in wrapround Ralph Lauren home furnishings "people wanted to put entire room sets on their charge cards, and just pantechnicon everything to the home counties, from the Edwardian-style bathrooms that look as though the Windsors have just popped out, to bedrooms Biggles would have been happy to crash into." wrote British *Vogue*.

Homewares was just another part of the fantasy lifestyle. But no one other than Lauren had such a commercial handle on it all, or had yet seen it as being part of one and the same world. "It's looking good and feeling good and being intelligent and standing for a good way of being in the world." explained Lauren, likening the ethos behind his home collections to that of his womenswear collections. "When that model came down the runway [in fall 1982] in the patchwork skirt and the pictorial sweater with the school and the kids and the tree across the front, and Neil Diamond was singing 'Hang on to the dream' – that was everything I believe in, everything I am."

"I DON'T USUALLY FEEL COMFORTABLE WALKING IN TO DESIGNERS' STORES. AT RALPH EVERYBODY MAKES YOU FEEL AT HOME."

VALENTINO

"SPORTSWEAR IS ABOUT
LIVING, AND THAT'S
WHERE AMERICA HAS
MADE ITS MARK."

RALPH LAUREN

THE SPORTING LIFE

In 1989, American *Vogue* boasted the coverline: "Fitness: changing the shape of fashion." It was to usher in an era of workouts, fitness regimes, and sports stars. Supermodels rushed to be the next Jane Fonda, with Cindy Crawford and Elle Macpherson making exercise videos to show women how to get the perfect body. The first Crunch fitness studio opened in New York, offering "Abs, Thighs, and Gossip" given by a drag queen instructor, as well as more conventional classes for upscale Manhattanites.

Meanwhile, women's sports were taking center stage for the first time, and the pages of glossy magazines were filled with shots of female volleyballers, tennis players, and golfers. Over time, these new heroines would slip onto the pages once reserved for celebrities. "Their rise to high profile status isn't thanks to sporting prowess alone, but because they have a face, and more importantly, a body, that fits the moment," wrote Mimi Spencer in British *Vogue*, referring to volleyball stars like Gabrielle Reece. "Ralph Lauren put it succinctly at the opening of his latest retail venture, Polo Sport: 'Health spas, good healthy food, working on your body – that's the real fashion of the Nineties.'"

Celebrating Lauren's love of the outdoors, and a belief in the value of staying fit, the Nineties ushered in an era of active fashion, whether it was running, racing, or even –in Lauren's tartan shirt and beige pants– fishing. British Vogue *wades in with this photograph by Arthur Elgort in 1990.*

Polo Sport, a new line of performance-based activewear launched in 1993, was the perfect fit for this newfound enthusiasm. With the handsome male model Tyson Beckford (the first African-American model to sign an exclusive contract with the brand) fronting its campaigns for the Polo Sport fragrances, later joined by part-Cherokee model Bridget Hall, the label epitomized health and vitality. The clothes came with the trademark stamp of Ralph Lauren authenticity, with Lauren the perfectionist collaborating with Reebok to make Polo Sport athletic shoes. As he would later go on to say: "You need function, but why not meld it with style?"

This was no fly-by-night fashion fixation; this trend was here to stay. "It seems as if everyone is racing, biking or stretching," wrote Mark Holgate in British *Vogue*. "And if they're not, then at the very least they're zipping, pulling and lacing themselves into sportswear.

While fashion has been conducting an affair with all things active for some time now nearly everyone is limbering up, thanks to sport's new found status." Here was a new generation, working hard and playing hard, in style. And even when neither work nor play but just lounging was required, suddenly the right kit was needed to do it in, or as Joan Juliet Buck wrote in *Vogue*: "It explains the over-whelming popularity of leotards and sweatpants and running shorts among people who are only thinking of exercising. Sweatpants are to women what cowboy boots are to men, a badge of hard work, of physical exertion, worn to prove that one has sweated, just as the boots are worn to prove one has been near a horse, a prairie, or that esteemed symbol of reality, the great Southwest."

Seemingly there was no sport you couldn't perform better without Lauren's performance-enhancing clothes. You could hit a searing tee shot with a Polo-logo'd golf ball, and be sure that golf pro Tom Watson, competing in Polo Golf clothes and starring in the campaign, would be doing the very same thing, albeit a little more skillfully. The scary colors and polyester fabrics that had been so much a part of golf were replaced by modern refined clothes in elegant fabrics like soft marl cotton, and elastane-enriched jersey. Polo Sport would accomplish the same sartorial achievements for several other sports. You might not be Wimbledon standard but the smart navy-blue and white Polo Ralph Lauren tennis balls would at least have you playing with style. As Lisa Armstrong noted in *Vogue*, "They [Polo Sport clothes] are beautiful enough to make an acrophobic take up mountaineering." By 1998, Lauren would take it one step further, launching RLX, a line of professional-quality athletic-wear for men and women, and would sponsor a World Cup mountain bike team, national world champion triathletes, and even snowboarders.

If Lauren's leisurewear was the unofficial uniform for those in pursuit of a sporty-looking life, now it would become the official uniform too. The original mesh shirt for men, launched in 1972 and featuring the famous polo player logo, was redesigned to become the official tennis shirt for the US Open in 2005.

Beachwear for swimming —or even running—in as modeled by Stephanie Seymour in this shot by Patrick Demarchelier for American Vogue, *1989.*

*Model Niki Taylor leads
the troops in a stylish red
Ralph Lauren Activewear
soft stretch jumpsuit,
photographed by Max
Vadukul for American
Vogue in 1991.*

previous pages *The decade
that saw the rise of the
supermodels coincided with
the decade of being superfit.
Naomi Campbell sports a
beaded beige bikini (left) in
this photograph by Robert
Erdmann for British
Vogue, 1996.
Bridget Hall, Lauren's
campaign face for his sports-
oriented Polo Sport label,
works out in silver leggings.
(right). Photographed in
1996 by Sante D'Orazio.*

"CLOTHES FOR
EVERY DAY,
CLOTHES FOR
PLAY, CLOTHES
FOR LIVING
AS OPPOSED
TO OUTFITS
FOR SPECIAL
OCCASIONS
OR WORK."

RALPH LAUREN

How to play croquet: first,
pick Jacquetta Wheeler for
your team; second, a silk
sweater and pleated satin
skirt is the only way to win.
Photograph by Arthur Elgort
for British Vogue, 2004.

The unofficial uniform of the tennis enthusiast (left), photographed by Arthur Elgort for American Vogue in 1990, was to become the official uniform for both the US Open and Wimbledon (above), here caught by Julian Broad for British Vogue in 2007. "It embodies elegance and classicism – elements that are at the core of my creative vision," said Lauren.

Paying more than mere lip service to the sport it's made for, Ralph Lauren's skiwear is worn by skiers with an almost cultlike devotion, loved for its functionality as much as its form. Photographed by Arthur Elgort for British Vogue, 1996.

"BEAUTIFUL ENOUGH TO MAKE AN ACROPHOBIC TAKE UP MOUNTAINEERING."

His uniforms for Wimbledon officials a year later were also rapturously received. All on-court personnel, including umpires, line judges, and 200 ball boys and girls stepped out onto the hallowed grass courts of southwest London wearing preppy striped blazers, cable-knit sweaters, and gaucho pants or full skirts. The traditional colors— royal purple and Bentley green—were set off with the Wimbledon crest. "Wimbledon is a sporting event rooted in English tradition," explained Lauren. "It embodies elegance and classicism – elements that are at the core of my creative vision."

At the 2012 Olympics, the American team stepped into the stadium wearing a Ralph-Lauren-designed uniform for the second Olympics running (Lauren had also designed uniforms for the winter games in Vancouver in 2008). His sleek preppy navy blazers, crisp pants, knee-length skirts, and jaunty caps embodied the same design principles as the main Ralph Lauren collections. The Olympic uniform was not without controversy; in spite of the fact that prior to Lauren's involvement the uniforms had not been made in the USA, Lauren was criticized for outsourcing his manufacturing to China. No one had complained before, but with the American economy still recovering from a downturn, there was now an outcry. Team Lauren was quick to rectify the situation, promising that while it was too late to do an about-face for the 2012 Olympics, the next batch, due for winter 2014, would be made on home turf. After the uproar, the *New York Times* noted, "Perhaps it would be simpler to go back to the ancient tradition of competing in the buff."

Lauren's personal enthusiasm for putting the sports back into sportswear came from his love of running, riding, and tennis. But since a health scare in 1987, a new awareness for the importance of staying fit had become apparent and with it came a more urgent appreciation of the sporting life. In *Vogue*, Buck wrote: "In the spring of 1987, a tumour was found in [Lauren's] brain; he waited until after his show to have it removed. It proved benign but left him with a scar along his hairline and a small mark on his forehead. He does not like to talk about either the experience or its consequences, but he had

come up against pain, uncertainty, mortality. When he returned to work, he made sleek, fast, simple clothes, which he said were inspired by his collection of classic racing cars, and he danced on the runway when the show was over."

These "sleek, fast, simple clothes" were the inspiration for a new way to do sportswear, the umbrella term used to describe everything from casual tweed jackets and mannish-looking shirts, to jeans, eveningwear, and coats. "When I was growing up people dressed for the weekends the way they did during the week," said Lauren, explaining the emergence of lifestyle clothes. "It wasn't until American life evolved and people started moving to the suburbs and having cookouts and enjoying more free time that there was a need for more comfortable clothes. I was creating American sportswear – clothes for every day, clothes for play, clothes for living as opposed to outfits for special occasions or work. Sportswear is about living, and that's where America has made its mark."

As he had quietly been observing, there were increasing numbers of women around with money and good figures who wanted to wear informal clothes with a strong fashion message. With the invention of lycra in 1959, wholeheartedly embraced by Americans in a way that Europe was yet to catch on to. Lauren now incorporated sleek, body-conscious lines into his designs for eveningwear and daywear that would show off fit, toned bodies. Elegant column dresses in form-fitting fabrics, all-in-one unitards —occasionally it was hard to see where clothes for sports began and sportswear left off; but one thing was for sure, you needed to be fit to wear them. Here were evening dresses that clung to every curve, eschewing the frills and formality of more traditional eveningwear in favor of something less ostentatious but no less striking and powerful. Sometimes sleek in satin, sometimes cowl-backed, sometimes strapless. Lauren launched a new period of glamorous, understated eveningwear that nonetheless remained true to its sportswear roots.

On board in nautical style, a skintight cotton jersey dress with a striped bodice is worn under a seafaring, fitted double-breasted blazer with gilt buttons. Photograph by Neil Kirk for British Vogue, 1992.

overleaf Paolo Roversi's atmospheric rendition for British Vogue in 1984 of nautical swimwear (left) is a classic example of Lauren's belief in form being an essential component of function. A form-fitting column dress shows off a toned physique (right), while allowing movement, even on a muddy American football pitch. Photograph by Bruce Weber for American Vogue, 1997.

This was something that was often picked up on by *Vogue*'s photographers over the years. Steven Klein pictured a model lifting up a truck, while wearing a gold form-fitting Ralph Lauren Collection dress. In 1989 Herb Ritts photographed supermodel Tatjana Patitz in a velvet strapless and seamless sheath, for which the caption duly noted: "One outcome of the athletic Eighties: dresses cut to show the body at its best." More recently Patrick Demarchelier captured model Joan Smalls in a pleated gold lamé dress, running alongside a mural of sprinter Usain Bolt. These were dresses that made a woman look strong.

For day, Lauren took his classic tank and T-shirt shapes and adapted them into figure-flattering dresses. "The spring silhouette is pared down to its purest form, with simple, sculptural lines that mould the body," he said, of his ankle-grazing T-shirt dress which had a body-hugging sensuality thanks to its cut on the bias from matte jersey. There were dresses for every occasion and no occasion. If you wanted to rock up to a beachside party, here was a long tank dress you could roll into a ball and take in your hand luggage: no ironing required. Need something elegant yet comfortable for après-ski? An ankle-length cashmere dress in soft gray would take the T-shirt shape in a new direction. Even the humble polo shirt was given a makeover with a new incarnation and an appropriately fitness-orientated moniker: the Skinny. It had a narrower fit and came in a hundred colors (plus the option of customization). "They remind me of M&Ms," said Lauren. "The colours are really fresh and the shape opens up a whole new realm of ways to wear it – it works just as well with heels and a mini as it does with a pair of shorts."

Understated eveningwear that is modern and powerful: Cindy Crawford models a classic Polo Ralph Lauren black cashmere halterneck sheath dress that stays true to its roots in sportswear. Photographed by Arthur Elgort for British Vogue, 1995.

Lauren had often drawn inspiration from sports for his main collections. As *Vogue* put it after his spring 1992 show: "Lauren stole the uniforms he designed for the America's Cup America racing syndicate right off the helmsman's backs, opening his show with a series of bright green, red, blue, and yellow leather anoraks, windbreakers and four-alarm coats with big brass buckles. Worn with sleek cobalt or red bodysuits, gold platform loafers, and jaunty yachting caps, they set the tone for a focused collection of all-American sportswear – Lauren's forte."

"DRESSES CUT TO SHOW THE BODY AT ITS BEST."

VOGUE

Joan Smalls runs alongside a mural of sprinter Usain Bolt in a pleated gold lamé dress, photographed by Patrick Demarchelier for American Vogue in 2012.

Critics also observed with approval that he was borrowing from swimwear, and with the use of navy and ivory contrasts seemed almost to be paying tribute to the breezy ease of Coco Chanel.

Likewise, his equestrian collection of 1985 was a marriage of Lauren's love of riding and English traditional riding habits. Chic Manhattanites would eagerly slide into their jodhpurs and "head for the Claremont Riding Academy on the Upper West Side, where the 10am Sunday class is perennially popular before brunch at Mortimer's"—wrote British *Vogue*. The riding influence would later extend to feature a stirrup on his watch collection. ("The very tool that revolutionised the way we ride horses – changing everything from medieval warfare to transportation to modern sports – is now elevating the way we tell time," wrote British *Vogue*, adding mischievously, "OK, the diamonds are a big help too").

Like the diamonds on the stirrup, Lauren would make even a T-shirt feel expensive, either by the cut or the choice of soft marl cotton, or the store in which it was sold. "No designer has eulogized the practicality or the romance of a T-shirt and jeans more than Ralph Lauren," wrote Holgate in *Vogue*. "Yet despite the authentic appeal of many of the details and finishes, the power of his clothes also lies in the fact that they are utterly luxurious. For all their outdoors image, they are meant for urban living, not riding the rodeo or doing a tour of duty overseas. And the price tag reflects this."

Lauren would apply the same rule of luxe-meets-practicality to his mens' label, Double RL, named after his Colorado ranch, in turn named after his and Ricky's initials. Launched the same year as Polo Sport, Lauren's new label introduced luxurious vintage looks in new, high-quality separates, with the kind of clothes that seemed like they'd been lived in by the likes of such American icons as Steve McQueen or Katharine Hepburn; classic American outdoor gear presented as rough-and-tumble clothes cowboys and farmers might wear, clothes for people who do things, even if they were more likely to be worn at weekends by casually dressed Manhattanites at their home in Montauk.

"YOU NEED FUNCTION, BUT WHY NOT MELD IT WITH STYLE?"

RALPH LAUREN

A velvet-collared Douglas jacket, tartan wool cape, and cotton velvet leggings are the quintessential getup for the best-dressed rider. Photograph by Hans Feurer for British Vogue, 1991.

His Ralph line, launched in 1999 with its speedy sharp design and reinterpretation of classics, proved to be a massive hit with a younger customer. He applied the same principles to his new look sportswear that he'd always used: rugged simplicity, utilitarianism, a masculine edge, relaxed yet robust enough for whichever of Lauren's worlds you wanted to visit. Chambray shirts, jackets that had their roots in naval and army uniforms (Lauren had a vast personal collection of original pieces), Western-inspired workwear, or chino pants were about to become the uniform of an active generation. "That's what's cool about Lauren, this simple elegance," wrote André Leon Talley in *Vogue*. "Everything pared down, then hit with a dash of luxury."

And yet, even for a designer with Lauren's vision, there were surprises in store for his rendition of sportswear. The casual form-meets-function look of his menswear lines had an unexpected following that started during the 1980s, proving to be a hit with the Lo-Lifes, a gang from some of Brooklyn's harshest projects who achieved notoriety for raiding department stores for highly collectable Polo and Polo Sport clothes, then wearing them as a uniform. They took their name from the "Lo" in "Polo." "The young men did everything in their power to attain as much of the clothing as they could, and treated the streets, clubs and subways of New York in the late 80s and early 90s as their catwalk," wrote John McDonnell in the *Guardian* newspaper. From bright yellow rain suits designed for fishing to his skiing and polo-playing outfits, the Lo-Lifes appreciated both the clothes (however incongruous they might look on the street corners of Brooklyn) and the man behind them, because of his humble beginnings. Other designers were quick to see the commercial potential. In the late 1980s Isaac Mizrahi designed a hip-hop inspired collection and in the 1990s Tommy Hilfiger would send rappers P. Diddy and Coolio down his catwalks. Once again, Lauren was ahead of his time. Never mind how enthusiastic the world of fashion was for Lauren's sportswear-for-lifestyle looks; in hip-hop culture, Ralph Lauren was cool.

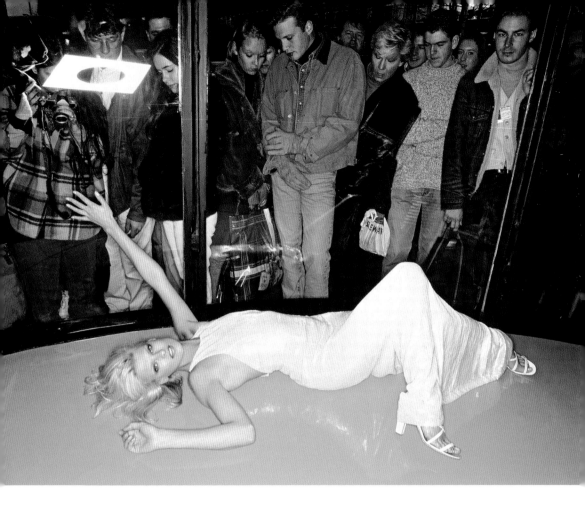

On display, Linda Evangelista in an
ivory sequined column dress and
grosgrain sandals, photographed by
Nick Knight for British Vogue, 1995.

overleaf Paolo Roversi's striking
portrait (left) of a model in a Ralph
Lauren red riding jacket, for British
Vogue, 1985.
Two stirrup watches and silk riding
scarves (right) are a timely reference
to the designer's love of all things
equestrian, the diamonds bordering the
watch adding more than just a touch
of luxury. Photograph by Mark Mattock
for British Vogue, 2009.

"RALPH LAUREN HAS NEVER
TRIED TO BE ANYTHING
THAT IT DIDN'T START OUT
TO BE. THAT SINGULARITY
IS WHAT BUILDS GREAT
BRANDS, BRANDS THAT LAST
AND BRANDS THAT YOU
ALWAYS REMEMBER."

PHILLIP LIM

BILLION-DOLLAR BRAND

On Valentine's Day, 2013 Ralph Lauren presented his Fall collection, one of the key shows of New York Fashion Week. Out filed the models, one in a reworked Aran sweater, fitted close to the body and teamed with a full-length taffeta and organza black skirt, others in romantic dresses with plenty of Lauren's movie-style magic, as well as other highlights: a delectable quartet of jewel-toned velvet dresses; an off-white shearling jacket (Ralph Lauren stopped using real fur in 2006; the sheepskins used for shearling being the exception). There was also, as there is in every Ralph Lauren show, something entirely new: in this case, a sleeveless black dress made from pleated silk and leather. Fifty-six years previously, a young Ralph Lauren had written in his end-of-school yearbook in 1957, in the space reserved to sum up his future career, just one word: Millionaire. In 2013, with 371 directly operated stores, as well as 488 concession store locations, fifty-eight licensed stores internationally, and around 30,000 employees, it's safe to say that this is a box he ticked a long time ago.

It's often said among industry insiders that whatever aspect of the fashion industry you're interested in, Ralph Lauren is the model. But Lauren's was no overnight success story; more a tale of hard graft, marketing genius, and risk-taking. The small company that began with a line of wide ties now straddles the very top of the fashion establishment, outranking other big commercial names such as Calvin Klein, Donna Karan, and Giorgio Armani. But, if this was something he'd envisaged all those years ago, then there were times when he must have seriously doubted his chances of its becoming a reality.

In 1972, when Polo was grossing $10 million, the women's line was launching, and he had won his first Coty Award, rumors were rife that he was going bust. "I was shivering," he said in American *Vogue* in 1982. "Designers usually don't start a company and then try to run it – I'd done it all backwards." The problem was, he'd grown too fast, doubling in size in too short a time. Even Bloomingdales, his first big account, had to send him checks in advance so that he could complete his women's collection and pay his bills.

"THEY REMIND ME OF M&MS. THE COLOURS ARE REALLY FRESH."

RALPH LAUREN

The shirt on which an empire was built. Lauren was shrewd enough to realize early on that a high-end image with a lower-priced entry-point was essential to ensure worldwide reach for the house. Carmen Kass models the cashmere version of the Black Label Polo shirt, photographed for American Vogue in 2000 by Mario Testino.

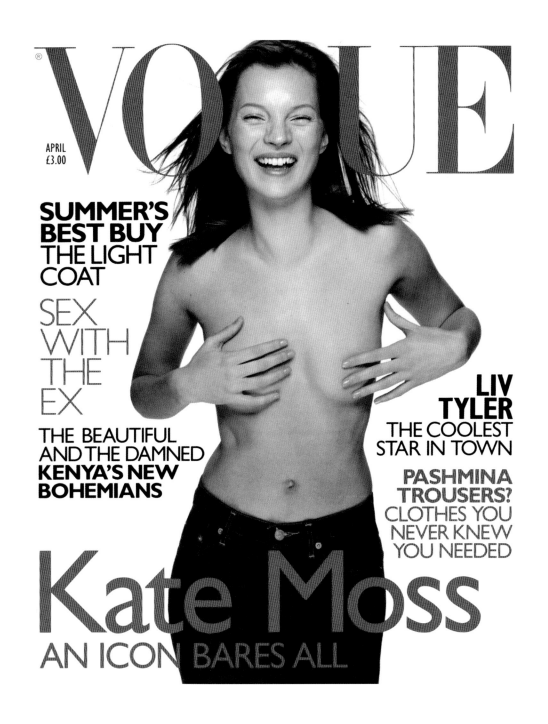

VOGUE

APRIL
£3.00

**SUMMER'S
BEST BUY**
THE LIGHT
COAT

SEX
WITH
THE
EX

**THE BEAUTIFUL
AND THE DAMNED
KENYA'S NEW
BOHEMIANS**

**LIV
TYLER**
THE COOLEST
STAR IN TOWN

**PASHMINA
TROUSERS?**
CLOTHES YOU
NEVER KNEW
YOU NEEDED

Kate Moss
AN ICON BARES ALL

Knowing he had to act quickly to turn it all around, he put his savings of $100,000 straight into the business. He licensed out his womenswear, which allowed him to focus on the design but leave the running costs and distribution to an outside party. He then turned to Peter Strom, who worked for one of his early backers, and persuaded him to become his partner, a relationship which would last until Strom retired in 1995. Here was someone who could reorganize the business for him, with the support of his brothers Jerry and Lenny. Strom's role was to prove crucial in establishing efficient working structures and he immediately set up a regular schedule of payments and deliveries; he also eliminated two-thirds of their 600 or so accounts by insisting that if they wanted to carry the label they had to be able to sell the Polo suit, which in those days sold for around $350 (roughly the equivalent of $2000 today). This cemented the image of Ralph Lauren as a luxury brand and thus gave the label a preeminent position in what would soon become a more saturated and competitive market. It also helped to provide unity across the brand from perfume to paint to Polo shirts. The high-end image was maintained, but customers were able to buy in at a lower price point. Strom also instigated the opening of outlet stores—an innovation in the early 1980s, but now a common enough retail feature of most designers, allowing the house to control the sale of any items that hadn't sold by the end of the season. Lauren and Strom encouraged longevity and loyalty—anyone who stuck with the house experienced their commitment with employees trained to represent the image of Ralph Lauren in the same way across cultures.

Fashion constants: Kate Moss models Lauren's jeans. Denim has been a big seller throughout the forty-six years of Lauren's career, whether cut as robust workwear or worn as faded classics with a lived-in feel. Photograph by Nick Knight for British Vogue, *1999.*

overleaf *Demi Moore strikes a pose in a floor-skimming Ralph Lauren Collection beaded dress. Photograph by Mario Testino for American* Vogue, *2003.*

In 1994, the company would again be at the brink of bankruptcy, as too-rapid growth was made more difficult by distribution issues. An infusion of cash from Goldman Sachs, who purchased 28 percent of the company for $135 million saved the day, and also led to Lauren taking the Polo by Ralph Lauren group on to the stock market three years later, an option that was not taken lightly as this would mean losing a certain degree of control. Overnight, the shares rocketed.

"RALPH WAS ONE OF THE FIRST TO UNDERSTAND HOW CLOTHES ARE NOT ONLY FOR WEARING — THEY CAN CONJURE UP DREAMS OF A LIFE."

ALEXANDRA SHULMAN

This was a different world from the one in which Lauren had started out. "By the time Gucci, Donna Karan, and Ralph Lauren went public in the mid-Nineties, the climate of consumer culture had changed radically," wrote Katherine Betts in American *Vogue*. "The establishment as it had once existed – predicated on the notion of high and low aesthetics, those decrees from Paris – was increasingly irrelevant. Information – even taste – was democratized. For the first time, Middle America knew as much about Gucci's stock listing as it did about Tom Ford's latest snaffle-bit stiletto. Women had a much bigger choice and a much more complicated role in the global market – they could buy the shoe or shares in the company. Their aesthetic experience was liable to be informed by a lot of financial and lifestyle facts."

For a designer like Lauren, this was an easier footing on which to begin a new public-listed life. He had already put his lifestyle, his passions, and pursuits—from a love of interiors to his impressive vintage car collection—out there for everyone to see. You could call it clever marketing, but communicating to customers this way was practically a Lauren invention. Even with this advantage, Lauren had some serious competition just as the economy hit another downturn. While the clothes from his Collection line, his shows, and his glamorous advertising campaigns formed a relatively small part of his actual business (as with every designer), they were vital to drive the sales of his lower-priced and more profitable merchandise from his Polo Sport and other more casual lines. "His rivals in this area are Calvin Klein and Tommy Hilfiger," noted American *Vogue* in 1996.

Sixteen months after its opening on the stock market, the shares fell dramatically. Lauren's response was to keep to what he did best —he had never resorted to gimmicks, for example by trading on his popularity with the Lo-Lifes. He updated his eveningwear, expanding it to include more formal Oscar-worthy gowns, which became increasingly important as the power of celebrity endorsement rose.

Freja Beha Erichsen up a tree in a sequin and tulle ball gown demonstrates the designer's increasing popularity for red-carpet looks, as photographed for British Vogue by Corinne Day, 2006.

overleaf *The visualization in sketch form of Lauren's creation for Gwyneth Paltrow's Oscar dress. The designer works with a team of artists to bring his design vision to life. "Paltrow at the 1999 Oscars, wearing a Ralph Lauren dress that nearly became as much of a star as the star herself." So wrote American Vogue in 2002, of Gwyneth Paltrow's famous pale pink taffeta gown and wrap.*

Ralph Lauren
for
Gwyneth Paltrow
Academy Awards
1999

"RALPH LAUREN IS
TO ME THE ULTIMATE
AMERICAN DESIGNER,
AS HE MADE TRUE
AMERICAN STYLE,
NOT JUST FASHION,
ACCESSIBLE TO
EVERYONE IN THE
WORLD."

KARL LAGERFELD

VOGUE

APRIL
£3.40

**FASHION,
FOOD AND
FITTINGS**
Sharing
one model's
couture

**TRENDS
TRANSLATED**
A LOOK FOR
EVERY AGE

**JOSS
STONE**
Style siren

SUPER
EASY
GLAMOUR

**WHAT'S
HOT
WHERE**
Fashion's
map of
the world

The
New
A-Z
of
Jewellery

**SPRING
CLEAN
YOUR LIFE**

One such robe was famously photographed on a young Gwyneth Paltrow in 1999 when she collected her Oscar for Best Actress, for her role in *Shakespeare in Love*. Romance, a floral fragrance, was launched in 1998—it was an instant hit. He also appointed a new president and chief operating officer, Roger Farah, who looked at the supply chain and bought back some of the licenses the business had sold over the years, including Japan, South Korea, and China, thus giving the company more control over production and distribution.

Once again, crisis was averted and a period of new expansion began, with flagship stores opening in Milan, Paris, and Moscow and later, Tokyo. In New York, in 2010 a Beaux-Arts style mansion was built directly opposite the Rhinelander store at 888 Madison Avenue to rehouse his womenswear and home collections, leaving the Rhinelander store across the road to be wholly devoted to menswear. (Strangers have been known to accost him in the street and thank him for the sympathetic architectural additions to the neighborhood.)

Lauren's son David was brought in to keep the company's marketing fresh in 2000, running a new media company for his father and helping to navigate the digital world, producing online-only fashion shows ahead of other competing brands and building what started off as sluggish e-commerce sales into what has now become the brand's biggest "store" in America. David Lauren's 4D sound and light shows in the New York and London flagship stores in 2010 left onlookers open-mouthed in amazement. "Before a thousand eyes, the gracious Ralph Lauren store will seem to vanish from sight," wrote Suzy Menkes in the *New York Times*. "Then in the empty space, the mansion on London's New Bond Street is to re-emerge brick by brick, until the façade opens, to be filled by giant, striding models, four storeys tall, their rose-patterned skirts then morphing into beds of flowers." It seemed that in David, Lauren might have found a natural successor for when his current contract would expire in 2017.

"I HAVE A VISION FOR LIVING. IT'S ABOUT ELEMENTS OF STYLE. IT'S ABOUT ALL THE THINGS THAT I LOVE, THAT I BELIEVE IN."

RALPH LAUREN

Newlyweds David Lauren
and Lauren Bush, the niece
of president George W Bush,
in a gown designed by her
father-in-law, photographed
for American Vogue by
Norman Jean Roy, 2011.

previous page Dancing
the night away in their
Jamaican home, Ralph
and Ricky Lauren are
photographed by creative
collaborator and friend
Bruce Weber for American
Vogue, 2000.

"There are very few designers who have Ralph Lauren's genius when it comes to envisioning and controlling every aspect and expression of their brand." said Anna Wintour, American *Vogue* editor-in-chief. "It's never easy to be your own man and your father's son, but David is absolutely both."

Besides his family, the key to both his long past career and his buoyant future, were Lauren's team, many of whom had been there if not since the beginning then for ten, twenty, or even thirty years, something of an anomaly in the sometimes fickle, always fast-moving world of fashion. Backstage at the Fall 2013 show, as she'd been at every show since 1971, was his right-hand woman, Buffy Birrittella. "Tanned and blonde, she's an older version of the Ralph Lauren woman," wrote Mary Tannen in American *Vogue* (1996), while observing the design process of Lauren and his team. "His mind and hers work in tandem. He is instinct; she is reason. He works by sight and touch. She provides work for his sometimes imprecisely articulated thoughts. She also has a computer-like memory for every garment Ralph Lauren has ever produced. When she speaks it could be the other side of his brain joining in." Under Birrittella's guidance his design team has always managed to feed him new sketches, tear sheets from magazines past and present, vintage clothes, or Ralph Lauren archive fabrics—anything that might inspire further ideas, keeping everything coming under a steady flow.

Bruce Weber has fond memories of how Lauren always inspired the team, formed while working together on those advertising campaigns, to do their best, and paid tribute to them in *Vogue Paris*: "My team … art directors, fashion designers, house models and me would all strive to surprise and delight [Lauren] by putting in the scene things that pleased him." Lauren himself has never been motivated by purely commercial concerns: when he lost a close friend to breast cancer in 1990, he set up Fashion Targets Breast Cancer, partnering with the CFDA (Council of Fashion Designers of America) and worked with Memorial Sloan-Kettering Cancer Center and Harlem's North General hospital to create the Ralph Lauren Center for Cancer Care and Prevention.

More charitable causes would be embraced, encompassing everything from Aids charities to helping the Abyssinian Development Corporation which supports housing and education. Another cause close to his heart was his underwriting of the restoration of the Star-Spangled Banner to the tune of $13 million, the original flag said to have inspired the American national anthem, and certainly a source of design and lifestyle inspiration to him. "Few designers have been as generous as Lauren," said André Leon Talley in *Vogue*.

The awards and accolades have continued to roll in. By the time of his 40th anniversary, celebrated with a party in Central Park, he had racked up several Coty Awards for menswear, womenswear, and retailing. His peers were not shy of heaping praise: when Lauren collected his Legion d'Honneur from President Sarkozy in 2010, Karl Lagerfeld commented, "I have always admired and respected Ralph Lauren. He is to me the ultimate American designer, as he made true American style, not just fashion, accessible to everyone in the world ... Lauren is someone who always changes his brand because after five years, a brand can become boring ... His is never boring."

But perhaps the most poignant moment came in 1992, when Audrey Hepburn, an iconic figure to Lauren, who had always admired her style and watched all her movies, presented him with the 1991 CFDA Lifetime Achievement Award, the biggest award in the fashion industry. She gave a moving speech celebrating the achievements of Lauren in which she pointed out how hard it was to pin him down with mere words. His influence went far beyond selling clothes: "Ralph has given American design a distinctive point of view and dignity. He has done this so consistently that his name is often used as an adjective that is synonymous with quality and style. And if you say something is 'very Ralph Lauren' you are immediately understood." Ralph, she went on, had shown everyone a different way of looking at the world.

A new generation of star models displays Lauren's enduring black-and-white tailored chic: Rosie Tapner in a crepe shirtdress; Sam Rollinson in a buttoned jacket and wool skirt; Cara Delevingne in a jersey jacket, embroidered silk blouse, and crepe skirt. Photographed for British Vogue in 2013 by Angelo Pennetta.

previous pages Lauren has often emblazoned his clothes with the American flag. Tatjana Patitz in a racer-back black column dress (left) featuring the Stars and Stripes is photographed by Peggy Sirota for British Vogue, 1991.
A Stars and Stripes sweater celebrates the designer's love for the American icon. Photographed for British Vogue, 1989, by Paul Lange.

"I HAVE AN IMMENSE
RESPECT AND
PASSION FOR HIM
AND HIS WORK ...
TO BE FAITHFUL TO
HIMSELF IS THE ONLY
CHARACTERISTIC
THAT MAKES
THE DIFFERENCE
BETWEEN A GREAT
DESIGNER AND A
LESSER ONE."

VALENTINO

*The grand finale: Lauren
takes in the applause at the
end of a show.*

Index

Page numbers in *italic* refer to illustrations

References

Gross, Michael. *Genuine Authentic: The Real Life of Ralph Lauren*, HarperCollins, 2004

McDowell, Colin, *Ralph Lauren: The Man, the Vision, the Style*, Cassell Illustrated, 2002

Lauren, Ralph, *Ralph Lauren*, Rizzoli, 2007

Trachtenberg, Jeffrey A., *Ralph Lauren: The Man Behind The Mystique*, Little, Brown & Company, 1988

Picture credits

Author's acknowledgments:

With thanks to all at British *Vogue* for their input, but especially Brett Croft, Library and Archive Manager at Condé Nast, and to Jo Ellison for sprinkling the magic dust yet again. Seeing all the captivating images in one book, realizing all the hard work that goes into making each picture from teams of hair-stylists, makeup artists, stylists, models, photographers, editors, and art departments, is humbling: thank you. Thank you also to all at Ralph Lauren, but especially Mary Randolph Carter for inviting me into her tiny (albeit beautifully furnished) office and sharing her infinitesimal knowledge garnered over her long and brilliant career to help me edit the thousands of images down to the very special few gathered here. Finally, this book couldn't have been written without the original archive interviews and articles that paved the way. In particular I would like to thank all the great writers from *Vogue*—to name a few: Joan Juliet Buck, Jesse Kornbluth, Lisa Armstrong, Mark Holgate, André Leon Talley, Paul Rudnick— and elsewhere, who over the years have enlightened us all with their wit, warmth, and sheer hard work. It was a joy reading you, thank you.

First published in 2013 by
Quadrille Publishing Limited
www.quadrille.co.uk

Publishing Director Jane O'Shea
Creative Director Helen Lewis
Series Editor Sarah Mitchell
Series Designer Nicola Ellis
Designer Lucy Gowans
Assistant Editor Romilly Morgan
Production Director Vincent Smith
Production Controller Leonie Kellman

For *Vogue*:
Commissioning Editor Harriet Wilson
Picture Researcher Ben Evans

Library of Congress Control Number:
2014942813

ISBN: 978-1-4197-1589-1

Text copyright © 2013 Condé Nast Publications
Limited

Design and Layout © 2013 Quadrille Publishing
Limited

Published in 2014 by Abrams Image, an imprint of ABRAMS. All rights reserved. No portion of this book may be reproduced, stored in a retrieval system, or transmitted in any form or by any means, mechanical, electronic, photocopying, recording, or otherwise, without written permission from the publisher.

Printed and bound in China
10 9 8 7 6 5 4 3 2 1

Abrams Image books are available at special discounts when purchased in quantity for premiums and promotions as well as fundraising or educational use. Special editions can also be created to specification. For details, contact specialsales@abramsbooks.com or the address below.

Vogue Regd TM is owned by the Condé Nast Publications Ltd and is used under licence from it. All rights reserved.

ABRAMS
THE ART OF BOOKS SINCE 1949

115 West 18th Street
New York, NY 10011
www.abramsbooks.com